God's Amazing Intimacy in Grief,
Surviving the Loss of a Loved One

By Gina Marie Mordecki

God's Amazing Intimacy in Grief, Surviving the Loss of a Loved One

ISBN: 9798578563751 (paperback)

Printed in the United States of America

Dedication

This book is dedicated to my daughter Janessa Michelle Saunders. She has supported me through the writing process, believed in me, and encouraged me along the way. She is the sunshine in my life.

This book is also done to honor the memory of Jemma, loved by her family and friends.

Table of Contents

Preface

When my daughter was raped and murdered. I prayed "Lord, don't let Jemma's death be in vain. Let something good come from it." I believe this book is the answer to that prayer. I will take you through my heartache, and eventual healing. I believe it will help to heal the heart of anyone who has experienced the loss of a loved one.

Acknowledgements

I would like to thank my dearest friends who were willing to revisit the pain they endured when they too lost a child. They each shared a piece of their heart in hopes it would minister to hurting souls: Cheryl Duncan, Colleen McDaniels, Donna Knoblock, Gwenn Ricketts, JoAnn Dunn, and Lin Berman.

Special thanks to Lin Berman for always being there to read, reread, critique, and support me.

Thank you to all my friends and family for their financial support toward publishing this book.

Thank you to my sister-in-law Louisa Pandelli who covered me with prayer every step of the way. She is a faithful prayer warrior and one I can always count on.

I am most grateful to my Lord and Savior Christ Jesus, whose Spirit has guided me on this journey. He has shared His creative abilities with me. I could not have done it without the Lord in my life guiding me.

Chapter 1

God's Preparation

In 1999, my 22-year-old daughter was raped and murdered. The most common comment I heard after Jemma's death was, "I don't know how you deal with it". It was only by the grace of God I was able to function at all. The loss of my daughter can best be described by one word, sad. I felt sad everyday. I thought about Jemma from morning to night every day. I thought by returning to work I could escape the sadness and think of something besides how much I missed her, and longed to hold her and kiss her, but work didn't stop the sadness. I took one year off of work that turned into two years. I was raised in a home where you weren't supposed to cry. I remembered Jackie Kennedy Onassis and I tried to emulate her. I hid my tears in my pillow at night. I couldn't put Jemma's loss out of my mind or heart. I missed her warm smile. I missed hearing her say, "I love you mom", in the sweet tender way she always said it. I missed being able to call her up just to talk.

Jemma was affectionate. Sometimes she would greet me after work by meeting me in the garage before I could even get out of the car. She would say, "Hi mom!" with a big hug and a warm smile. In the house, she would plop down on the couch and put her arm around me and we would watch television together. I longed for those times.

Jemma was kind and trusting. She loved people and everyone loved her. She shouldn't have died like she did. Someone who loved her should have held her and been by her side.

After Jemma died, I said a prayer, "God, don't let Jemma's death be in vain, let something good come of it." Who would think a "God Story" could come of such horrific circumstances? Yet every time I told people how God gave me the strength to go on, they told me how deeply it impacted their life, often asking me to share my story with others.

Now I realize that God did hear my prayer. In

answering it, He has not only comforted me, but He has shown others just how intimate and loving a God He is.

***

"God is our refuge and strength, a very present help in trouble." (Psalms 46:1).

***

Long before Jemma was murdered, God began preparing both Jemma and me for the fate that awaited us. When Jemma was less than three years old, we were playing make believe tea party. She turned and matter-of-factly said to me, "Mom, I'm not going to live long, I'm going to die young". I didn't even know she had any conception of death. When a child so young says something like that, the words stay with you. Those words stayed tucked away in my memory bank. She repeated them two or three years later. We were in her room playing with her dollhouse. "Jemma! You are not going to die young!" Her reply was as matter of fact as before, "Yes I am". I thought to myself then, God are you trying to tell me something?

Every few years she echoed those same words. When she was eleven or twelve and said them, I asked her, "why do you always say that?" She answered as nonchalantly as always, "Because I am."

When Jemma was eighteen, she asked me to take an insurance policy out on her, again stating she was not going to live long. Taking my hand in hers, she said, "Mom, it's OK, I'm alright with it". I complied when the next insurance advertisement came through the mail.

Jemma went from winning 1st place in beauty pageants, blue ribbons in horse riding shows, 1st place in talent contests, doing a commercial on TV, good grades in school, to a lost and troubled girl.

***

When she was twenty-one, in September of 1998, she moved to Virginia. She wanted to get away from the negative influences around her. She had been using drugs and thought if she moved away she could make a new start. She called home every day to talk to her sister, my mother, or me.

In November, she came home for Thanksgiving. I remember like it was yesterday, looking at Jemma standing in the hall and saying to her, "Jemma, if you are ever in a life and death situation, where death is eminent, call out to Jesus and ask Him to forgive your sins and receive you into heaven". She answered, "Oh Mom". I said, "I mean it. Just like the thief on the cross."

***

Then one of the criminals who were hanged blasphemed Him, saying, "If You are the Christ, save Yourself and us." But the other, answering, rebuked him, saying, "Do you not even fear God, seeing you are under the same condemnation? And we indeed justly, for we receive the due reward of our deeds; but this Man has done nothing wrong." Then he said to Jesus, "Lord, remember me when You come into Your kingdom". And

Jesus said to him, "Assuredly, I say to you, today you will be with Me in Paradise" (Luke 23:39-43).

***

Jemma replied, "I know, I know, I will." Jemma had gone to a Christian school kindergarten through 6ᵗʰ grade and knew the teachings of Jesus. Little did I know how prophetic those words would be seven weeks later. On January 17ᵗʰ, 1999, Jemma was raped and murdered. Her lifeless body was found in an abandoned apartment five days later. Her murderer was discovered in her stolen car.

When you lose someone you love, your first thoughts turn to: Where is she now? Did she make it into heaven? Will I see her again? I began asking God for reassurances that Jemma was in heaven.

Chapter 2

Butterfly Love

O ne afternoon in June of 2000, two friends came over for a swim. We were sitting on the lower deck around the pool listening to music. A CD came on that my nephew had made in memory of Jemma. As we listened to the music, a bright orange butterfly began circling me. It was obviously trying to get my attention. I told the girls, "I'm going to the upper deck to see if she follows me". I climbed five steps to the upper deck, and sat in the corner where a built in bench lined the sides of the deck. I stretched out my legs down the left bench as my little butterfly companion lit on the left railing next to me. Thinking, this is not coincidence, I turned stretching my legs down the right side of the bench. The little butterfly came to light on the right railing. Then I placed a glass of soda I was holding on the small round table between the benches. The butterfly, wanting all my attention, came and lit next to my glass. The girls and I were in tears by now.

In no way do I think that that butterfly was Jemma. But I do believe that God sent her to confirm something to my heart. You see I believe in the transforming power of God's son, the Messiah, Christ Jesus. I believe when you ask Him into your heart, He will come in by way of His Holy Spirit and change your life. Thus, you become a new creation in Jesus.

***

"Therefore if anyone is in Christ, he is a new creation; old things are passed away; behold, all things have become new" (II Corinthians 5:17).

***

The analogy can be made by a caterpillar that goes into a cocoon and comes out transformed into a beautiful butterfly.

I got up and went to the steps, standing next to the railing. The butterfly followed lighting next to my hand that was resting on the railing. I told my friend Sharon that

I was going in to get a camera to take a picture with the butterfly. I stopped to say, "Sharon, this butterfly has a smile on its face!" "I know. I see it". "You see it too?" "Yes."

As I went inside to get my camera, I knew the butterfly would still be waiting when I returned. I almost took my time on purpose to prove it to myself. I returned with the camera. There she was, "Little Jemmie", as I came to call her. I showed Sharon what to do to work the camera. I put my finger next to Little Jemmie. I said, "Come on Little Jemmie, get on my finger." She climbed right up. I lifted my hand and held it next to my cheek and Sharon took the picture. It is not my best picture but I'm proud to show it.

Twice she flew away, approximately seventy to one hundred feet. Twice I called her back. "Come back Little Jemmie!" I didn't want the blessing to end. Twice she returned. Then my friend, Sharon, said, "May I hold her?" I said, "I don't know. Let's ask her." I instructed Sharon to put her finger out next to Jemmie as I asked, "Can Sharon hold you?" She flew away, never to return. It was my blessing, my intimate response from God. She was my Jemmie. She was God's Jemmie.

***

It was January 2002 when I was at a butterfly conservatory in Canada that I learned that butterflies don't have faces, smiley faces that is. They look very much like house flies. When I told an employee there my story, she asked me if I knew what the folklore was about butterflies. I didn't. She told me butterflies represent mothers and their children because they can't hurt you. They have no defense. Of course I cried as I walked amidst the butterflies in the conservatory. People probably thought I was crazy. I didn't care. I knew that God loved me enough to order the details of my life to comfort my hurts.

***

"The steps of a good man are ordered by the Lord: and he delights in his way" (Psalms 37:23).

Chapter 3

The Fish Dream

I'm one of those people who need a lot of reassurance. Even though I knew that Jemma knew the Lord and had asked Him into her heart, I wasn't sure what I believed about an issue Christians phrase, "Once saved, always saved". Let me explain. There are scriptures in the Bible that confirm that once you ask Jesus to come into your heart you are sealed by the Holy Spirit.

***

"In Him you also trusted, after you heard the word of truth, the gospel of your salvation; in whom also, having believed, you were sealed with that Holy Spirit of promise who is the guarantee of our inheritance until the redemption of the purchased possession, to the praise of His glory" (Ephesians 1:13-14).

***

These scriptures denote you belong to God; you have His seal upon you.

***

"And do not grieve the Holy Spirit of God, by whom you were sealed for the day of redemption" (Ephesians 4:30).

***

The day of redemption refers to when Jesus returns for his saints. Some will argue that you can lose your salvation by acts of unrighteousness. I wasn't sure if Jemma's lifestyle had kept her out of heaven. Again I went to God in prayer. This time I asked, "Lord, did Jemma call out to you in those last hours of her life like I told her to that day in the kitchen?"

I knew that God had given me those words to say to Jemma as much for me as for her, but did she say them?

***

Weeks later I was missing Jemmie, "Jemmie Lou" I liked to call her. I prayed and asked God for a dream so I could see my Jemma again, happy and vibrant. In a few days I had a dream. It wasn't the dream I prayed for. In fact I told God I hated it. It was awful. I also said, I know you are a loving father and if you gave me that dream there must be a good reason. Please give me the interpretation of it. Two days later I had the interpretation and with it the peace I needed once and for all that my Jemma was with the Lord.

***

"For God may speak in one way, or in another, yet man does not perceive it. In a dream, in a vision of the night,

13

when deep sleep falls upon men, while slumbering on their beds" (Job 33:14-15).

***

In my dream there were two rooms. I couldn't see clearly. It was as though I was looking through a fog. I knew that there was sexual perversion going on. I saw Jemma on her hands and knees. The only clear part of the vision was Jemma turning to face me with a blank expression on her face. She wasn't smiling. She opened her mouth and a big fish, like a rainbow trout, came out of her mouth. It was bigger than her head. Then I woke up.

I'm sure you can understand my disappointment over the dream I had. I waited to hear from God. "What are you trying to tell me?" Then it came to me. In my conscious mind God spoke to me. He reminded me how when Christian followers of Jesus traveled through the land, they had to be careful not to reveal their faith or they risked persecution. They might even be put to death. To keep their belief a secret, as they passed along a dirt path in their travels and encountered a stranger, they would draw an arc in the dirt. If the other person was a believer he would draw an arc over it, or under it, to look like the fish we often see on necklaces and bracelets or on cars. Then they knew it was safe to talk to each other. God spoke to my heart, "when Jemma was being raped and murdered she was calling out to Me, that is why in my dream the fish was coming out of her mouth."

I said, "Father I love the dream you gave me. If I would have had a beautiful dream with rainbows and flowers I might of thought it was something I dreamed up. This is not a dream I would ever have dreamed up. I know it came from you. Thank you Lord for your faithfulness and your love."

God doesn't promise a life without hardships. On the contrary, sometimes hardships are the only way God can get our attention. He does promise He will be there to help us through our trials.

My hope is that Jemma's story will help more people realize how close God's presence is, how much He loves us and wants to be a part of our lives. We have only to cry out to Him. He is there. He will never leave us or forsake us.

***

Let your conduct be without covetousness; be content with such things as you have. For He Himself has said, "I will never leave you or forsake you" (Hebrews 13:5).

You will find Him if you search for Him with all your heart.

***

"And you will seek Me and find Me, when you search for Me with all your heart" (Jeremiah 29:13).

***

I'm nobody special. I am just one of His children. He'll be just as intimate with anyone else who seeks Him with his whole heart. In the following pages, I will share scriptures with you, and share how the Lord was intimate with many of the women who passed through the grief meetings I hosted in my home and at the church I attended.

Chapter 4

Healing Through Communication

Two years would pass before I finally came out of the fog of grief. I didn't realize I was in a fog until it lifted. I functioned but there was always an ache in my heart. I thought about Jemma all day, every day, as I went about my daily routine. My heart felt like it was literally broken. I had an ache under my breast bone that was so real I had three EKG's, three stress tests, and a heart catheterization over the next five or six years. All the tests came back negative. The doctor told me you are suffering from a broken heart. The pain of a broken heart is literal. There was no other explanation but that the pain I was feeling was the hurt that came from losing my Jemma. Years later my mother died and that same pain came back. It's not unusual for people to become ill after losing someone. Emotional stress plays havoc on our bodies.

***

In 2002, I moved from Ohio to Florida. I needed sunlight to lift my spirits. I started attending a grief group that was offered in my church. It was just what I needed. I met other women who were just as broken as I was. As we met every week and shared our pain, something wonderful was happening. We were healing. Every week we were given the opportunity to talk about our loved one, cry, laugh, and share pictures. It was amazing. People really cared enough about my hurt and loss to let me talk about it. They cared enough about me to learn what losing Jemma meant to me.

When you lose someone close to you, many people don't know what to say to you, so they may not say anything. Some may attempt to console you, but no matter what they say you may not receive it the way they intended it. Because we knew that each of us were feeling that same deep hurt in our souls, we were able to accept what each other said. Sometimes we laughed, sometimes we cried, but we loved on each other week after week. Attending the grief meetings you feel protected to express whatever you feel. No one is there to judge you.

One of the best suggestions I can personally give a grieving parent is to get in a group with other grieving parents, preferably women with women and men with men. Sometimes spouses don't feel free to express their true feelings with their partner in the same room. They may not be ready for fear of hurting them, or may just need more time.

You may have to go to different grief groups in your city until you find the one that fits your needs. Please don't give up just because you are unhappy with the first one you go to. There may always be that one person who annoys or offends you, but realize they are grieving too and that will help you. You will feel more comfortable as time goes by. You don't have to talk. You can listen until one day you feel like talking. You can Google Grief groups to find one near you. You can meet together on line and eventually in person.

Many people are not ready to go to a grief group for the first few weeks, or sometimes few months. I couldn't really start grieving until the murder trials were over and that took two years. The perpetrator was a serial rapist. I went to the trials of the other woman that he had stabbed eleven times and raped, and then his trials for my daughter's murder before I could start grieving.

How long you go to grief meetings will depend on you. I went until I felt peace in my heart and continued longer to help other women who were just starting to come. It's nice to continue to go even after you heal because with the new women being at different levels of healing, we were able to give them hope. Helping others fills your own heart with gratification. I eventually started to facilitate the group.

Sometimes after a loss it is hard to return to church. I have had mothers who said all they could do was cry the whole time while sitting in church, so they decided to stay home. One mother could barely get off her couch for three months. No need to feel guilty, you will get there when you are ready. God will meet you where you are.

A word of caution, when Jemma was murdered, I was searching for comfort. I tried anti-depressants but they made me ill. I saw a psychiatrist once, but I wasn't comfortable. Then I decided to go to a support group for mothers of murdered children. There I was met with a spirit of anger and bitterness. Sadness permeated the atmosphere. It's been said that when you hate, it's like taking the poison pill you wanted to give the other person and swallowing it yourself. You are the one who has the stomach pain and the suffering. They don't feel your hate, pain, or even care about it. I'm not judging them for their anger, we can only do what we believe is right. I just want to say there is a better way, a healthier way.

I was fortunate in that I felt an instant forgiveness for the murderer. I know you think, how could you? It was only God's grace that made that possible. I am not saying I didn't want him to pay for his crime. I certainly did. I opted for a life sentence instead of death. He got nine life sentences and will never see the light of day. In my heart, I felt like being locked up in a cell forever was worse than death. I took a per diem job as a medication nurse in a prison briefly to learn what that might feel like. It was very dark, depressing, and gloomy. I learned what I needed to know.

Most importantly, communicate with God. Communicate in prayer. Remember to sit quietly and wait and let Him communicate with you. When you are talking with a friend you don't say everything you want to say and walk away. You give them a chance to respond. Give your Father time to respond. Most people who don't hear from God aren't giving Him a chance to speak. He's not likely to talk out loud. It will be a still quiet voice in your heart. Sometimes I know its God because what I'm hearing is smarter than me, other times my conscience just can't get it out of my head. It does take practice to hear His voice. I promise you He does want to talk with you. You are His child. He created you. Just like you love to hear from your children, He loves to hear from you.

***

The day before Jemma left for Virginia, I kept hearing in my head, "Tell Jemma to sleep with you". After having that thought come into my head so many times

I thought it must be God, so I reasoned with Him in my head, I was saying, "But I'm married, I sleep with my husband". I passed it off eventually and didn't act on it. Had I acted on it, I would have held my Jemma in my arms and slept with her the last night I would see her. I had fallen away from God at that time so my spiritual senses were not so keenly aware. I learned a big lesson. Jemma's death drew me back to God and now I am more alert to His voice. Learning to hear the voice of God does take time. Let Him communicate with you by reading the Bible. It is the inspired Word of God. Through the Holy Spirit, God guided man what to write. I suggest reading Psalms. I think it may be all I read for a year. It is one of the easiest and most comforting books to read, especially when you are feeling sad. God inspired the Bible; so God is speaking directly to you. Wouldn't you like to know what the creator of the universe, your heavenly Father, has to say? It's impactful. You will know the comfort only knowing God can bring. There is no one who can comfort you like Jesus; like God.

"All scripture is given by inspiration of God, and is

profitable for doctrine for reproof, for correction, for instruction in righteousness" (2 Timothy 3:16).

***

"Call to Me, and I will answer you, and show you great and mighty things, which you do not know" (Jeremiah 33:3).

Chapter 5

Why?

People often ask, "Why did they have to die?" Most of us are really saying, "Why now? Like this?" God is infinite. His thoughts and ways are higher than ours. God has a much bigger picture than we can wrap our finite minds around. With God, a day is like a thousand years, and earth is but the dressing room for heaven.

***

"For My thoughts are not your thoughts, nor are your ways My ways," says the Lord. "For as the heavens are higher than the earth, so are My ways higher than your ways, and My thoughts than your thoughts" (Isaiah 55:8,9).

***

Sometimes the death of our loved one is the instrument God uses to help us see His plan. Most of us would never think of the future in terms of dying until someone we love dies. Then we are forced to think about death. God has a reason for everything. We may not get to know the reason this side of heaven, but we can still pray for understanding.

***

"But, beloved, do not forget this one thing, that with the Lord one day is as thousand years, and a thousand years as one day" (II Peter 3:8).

***

(1) "To everything there is a season. A time for every purpose under heaven:

(2) A time to be born, and a time to die; A time to plant and a time to pluck what is planted;

(4) A time to weep and a time to laugh; a time to mourn and a time to dance" (Ecclesiastes 3:1, 2, 4);

***

Verse one states there is a purpose for everything God allows and a time for that purpose. God sees a much bigger picture. Look at the sky, and the galaxies beyond the sky. God created it all. He has big plans for all of us that extend far into eternity. God didn't create man with the intention that he should live awhile and die never to be seen again.

In the Garden of Eden, God gave man a choice.

***

"And the Lord God commanded the man, saying, of every tree of the garden you may freely eat; but of the tree of the knowledge of good and evil you shall not eat, for in the day that you eat of it you shall surely die" (Genesis 2:16,17).

God didn't mean die right then and there when they took that first bite. He meant man would eventually die on earth. His original plan was eternal life, but God wanted to give man a choice. God made man a free moral agent. He wanted to fellowship with a person who wanted to fellowship with Him. He didn't want robots forced to choose Him. Adam made a choice to eat of the tree of knowledge of good and evil, and so death came to earth. God knew man would fail. He had a plan for that.

God still gives man that same choice. Now there is no tree of life with fruit like in the garden, but there is a tree, with a Savior who came to hang and die on it to pay all of our sin debt in full.

***

"Who Himself bore our sins in His own body on the tree, that we, having died to sins, might live for righteousness—by whose stripes you were healed" (1 Peter 2:24).

We get another chance to get it right. We can choose the Savior, Messiah, Christ Jesus, or we can reject Him. If you choose Jesus, and make Him Lord and Savior of your life, you can have the eternal life God originally designed for us to have. It comes down to your choice. God never said we wouldn't die. When Adam and Eve ate that forbidden fruit, the death they experienced passed on to all the generations of people after them.

***

"Therefore, just as through one man, sin entered the world and death through sin, and thus death spread to all men, because all sinned" (Romans 5:12).

***

"But as many as received Him, to them He gave the right to become children of God, to those who believe in His name:" (John 1:12).

***

"For the wages of sin is death, but the gift of God is eternal life in Christ Jesus our Lord" (Romans 6:23).

***

When Jesus came to the earth to die as a sacrificial lamb to pay our sin debt in full, His death paid for the sins of all who choose Him. In the Old Testament Jewish people brought lambs to the temple as a sacrifice for their sins. Jesus's death was the last sacrifice for sins. When He died the temple split in two, those sacrifices stopped. They were no longer needed. Jesus fulfilled the scriptures. Jesus came to redeem mankind and give us hope, the hope of heaven, the hope of life eternal on a new earth.

It is this very hope that sustains you when you are going through grief. Without the hope of eternal life, the hope of seeing your loved one again, life would be empty.

Maybe you are like me, thinking did my son, my daughter, ever ask Jesus to forgive their sins, or invite Him to become their Savior. God promises in His Holy Word that He reveals Himself.

***

"For since the creation of the world His invisible attributes are clearly seen, being understood by the things that are made, even His eternal power and Godhead, so that they are without excuse" (Romans 1:20).

***

One can hardly look at the ocean with its massive waves breaking on the shore without seeing the hand of God, or look at a field of wild flowers blowing in the wind, or watch the sunset in hues of gold and orange afar off on the sea. It all speaks of God, the sky with all it's stars sparkling on a summers night, the snow capped mountains, the face of a newborn baby. Who can deny that there is a creator? Don't presume to know that on one of those beautiful sunny days that God wasn't speaking into the heart of your loved one.

***

Jesus said, "All that the Father gives Me will come to Me, and the one who comes to Me I will by no means cast out. This is the will of the Father who sent Me, that of all He has given Me I should lose nothing, but should raise it up at the last day. And this is the will of Him who sent Me, that everyone who sees the Son and believes in Him may have everlasting life and I will raise him up at the last day" (John 6:37, 39, 40).

***

Our loving Father wants the very best for us. I know it's not always easy to accept the things that happen in life, especially the loss of loved ones, but I promise you, God hurts when you hurt. He feels your pain. He came to earth as a man, Jesus, and experienced every pain you will ever feel. When you read the Bible and get to know your heavenly Father, Jesus, it will help you heal.

***

He promises to turn your mourning into dancing. (Psalms 30:11)

He will give you peace that passes understanding. (John 14:27)

He will give you the joy of the Lord to be your strength. (Nehemiah 8:10) and the garment of praise for the spirit of heaviness. (Isaiah 61:3)

***

If you have a hope, the hope of heaven, then you will know that you will see your loved one again. Yes, you will still suffer the pain of loss, but you will have the hope of eternity to spend with them. You will have the hope of seeing them again. This is only a temporary separation.

***

"But I do not want you to be ignorant, brethren, concerning those who have fallen asleep, lest you sorrow as others who have no hope" (I Thessalonians 4:13).

***

There is a purpose for everything, for everything that ever happens in our life. God doesn't waste one hurt or one tear.

***

"You number my wanderings; Put my tears into Your bottle; Are they not in Your book?" (Psalms 56:8).

***

"Precious in the sight of the Lord is the death of His saints" (Psalms 116:15).

Chapter 6

God's Comfort

After two years of attending a grief group at my church, I was asked to be a grief support leader. Due to space problems, we were eventually asked to host the meetings in our homes. At first I was reluctant, but soon realized that the warm, intimate atmosphere of a home seemed more conducive to sharing our hearts. For seven years, women whose child had died passed through my doors. We bonded and healed together.

Sitting in a circle around the living room we would share our heartaches, memories of our children, cherished pictures, and watch DVD's on overcoming grief. A small group of us have remained close friends till this day. I will share some of their stories and the ways God was intimate with each of them.

One such woman was Lin. She shared how God had prepared her well before her son went home to be with the

Lord. She had been in a Bible study group that had taught her to memorize scriptures. When she got the call that her son had died, those scriptures that she had memorized were the very scriptures she needed to get her through the initial shock. They came running through her mind.

As you can see, God can be intimate by preparing us ahead of time for what is about to take place. We don't always know God is preparing us until after the fact and we reflect back on things that happened or what we did, or heard.

***

"My son, give attention to my words; Incline your ear to my sayings, Do not let them depart from your eyes; Keep them in the midst of your heart; for they are life to those who find them, and health to all their flesh" (Proverbs 4:20-22).

***

After a season of grief meetings, perhaps two sessions

with the same women, I felt led to have a karaoke party. The women could bring their spouses and in some cases they already knew each other. I usually had the men come once during the 14-week program. We were singing karaoke songs and when a particular song came on that she and her husband used to dance to, he asked her to dance. We were blown away. They jitterbugged like the couples on Dancing with the Stars. They had met taking dance classes, but had not danced in two years. That night was deliverance for Lin. I saw her with tears in her eyes sitting on the couch. I asked her what was wrong. She said, "It's ok to have fun?" I replied, "of course it is". The bible says, "You have turned for me my mourning into dancing; You have put off my sackcloth and clothed me with gladness" (Psalms 30:11).

***

Lin and Fred started dancing and enjoying life again. God had truly turned their mourning into dancing.

***

"Then shall the virgin rejoice in the dance, and the young men and the old, together; For I will turn their mourning to joy, Will comfort them, and make them rejoice rather than sorrow" (Jeremiah 31:13).

***

Gwen lost her daughter, Jessica, to cancer. Today she blogs on her website, "Sisters From Another Mister", and also leads a Grief Share group. Like Lin, Gwen had studied scriptures for several years. She said one of the ways God ministered to her was when she was enjoying nature. As she pondered His creation, He would quicken her mind to a scripture she knew.

I know not everyone has a sound scripture base. Some people have very little knowledge of scriptures. If you are someone who hasn't spent much time reading the Bible, I encourage you to lean on God during this time and get to know Him by reading His Word. You will learn of His fervent love for you. As you read, He can make scriptures stand out to you to minister to you. I recommend the book of Psalms in the beginning. The scriptures are easy to understand and David, a King loved by God, wrote many of the Psalms after he lost his son from Bathsheba.

Cheryl, whose only son was taken by cancer, said that God met her need by bringing an old friend back into her life who had also lost a son. They bonded together again and were able to minister to each other.

Cheryl and her friend Mary both started coming to the meetings. Cheryl tells how her husband could not bear the thought of their son dying at home, saying he would never be able to walk past his room again. He was admitted to Hospice. The nurses would encourage them to stay all night but her husband wanted to leave at night. He could not endure to stay any longer. On the fourth night, the night her son died, she refused to leave. She reached out to hold his hand from the bed next to him and it was then that the Lord took him. When it was so important for Cheryl to be there both for her and her son, God saw to it that she stayed.

Mary became a special part of our family of mother's. She was a ray of sunlight in the lives of so many women. As she healed, she was able to take the group to her home and become a leader. Mary passed from cancer. She is fondly remembered by all of us.

Joanne came to the support group and said the DVD's we watched, together with the fellowship, were very helpful. She was quiet and didn't always have a lot to say but she knew she found a family of support.

Colleen's son, Jay, had struggled with addictive behavior starting in high school. He had been in and out of rehabs. About six months before Jay died, his sister had a dream that her husband had to wake her from as she was hysterically crying. Colleen said when her daughter told her about the dream, she felt as though the Lord might be preparing her for bad news. Six months later on his 36th birthday Jay died from a drug overdose in his sleep. God had used Jay's sister's dream to help prepare her mother.

Colleen became an advocate against doctors who were operating pill mills. She was instrumental in seeing their offices close by picketing in front of known drug mill offices.

Women who lose children often find solace by helping others. Many advocates of different programs stem from a broken heart and loss, just another way God uses our pain.

Donna's son Bryan lost his life in a battle with recreational drugs. To escape getting in trouble he swallowed the drugs. He had a heart attack in jail and was in the hospital on a ventilator for ten days. She and Bryan's father had the unhappy task of deciding when to unplug the ventilator. They left the room and went to the hospital lobby to get coffee and make their heart wrenching decision. As they entered the coffee shop, Bryan's favorite song came on, "Every Little Thing Is Going To Be Alright". God had made their decision easier. There are no coincidences with God.

God also showed up for Donna when she tossed the flower lei in the ocean where she had poured Bryan's ashes. The flowers made a heart and Donna had its image tattooed as a remembrance.

When Bryan was twelve years old he had a dream where he saw the things referenced in (Rev. 2:10), "Do not fear any of those things which you are about to suffer. Indeed, the devil is about to throw some of you into prison, that you may be tested, and you will have tribulation ten days. Be faithful until death, and I will give you the crown of life." In church that night while Bryan was leafing through his Bible, he motioned to Donna, excitedly, "Mom, mom, this is my dream." About six months after Bryan died Donna came across the scripture in her Bible and it ministered to her.

Mothers who lose their children from drugs often feel ashamed that their child had a problem with drugs. If you aren't famous and a part of the elite it often feels like society is unforgiving. These mothers love their children just as much as the mothers whose children die from cancer or some other disease. They really have nothing to be ashamed of. No one is perfect. We all have battles we fight.

In an attempt to comfort those who have lost someone to suicide, I would like to clarify what the Bible says regarding unforgiveable sins. There is only one sin that is unforgiveable according to the word of God. It is not suicide.

***

"Therefore I say to you, every sin and blasphemy will be forgiven men, but the blasphemy against the Spirit will not be forgiven men. Anyone who speaks a word against the Son of Man, it will be forgiven him; but whoever speaks against the Holy Spirit, it will not be forgiven him either in this age or in the age to come" (Matthew 12:31, 32).

***

People who suffer death by suicide are ill. They have not committed an unforgivable sin. Mental disorders affect your thinking, mood, and behavior; and they affect your actions. People die from suicide just like they die from heart disease. If they were able to think clearly or logically at the time they would not have acted on their impulse.

Chapter 7

Anger With God

Right now some of you might be saying, "I want nothing to do with God". I have heard that before. I can only remind you that death was not in God's original plan for man. When sin entered, death entered. We may not always agree with God's actions, but this is His plan. He is the creator. He is not obligated to get our approval for the way He carries it out. I don't mean for that to sound harsh. I know that when you lost your child, loved one, it was like the sunshine went out of your life. I understand that, but this really isn't how it ends, with your loved one in a grave. God is creating a new heaven and a new earth, one we cannot even imagine. Revelations 21 talks of that new heaven and new earth. I encourage you to read it.

Some people get a lot of comfort searching the words heaven and angels. You can search on the computer,

Google them, or use the concordance in the back of your Bible.

***

"Eye has not seen, nor ear heard, nor have entered into the heart of man the things which God has prepared for those who love Him" (I Corinthians 2:9).

***

"In my Father's house are many mansions, if it were not so, I would have told you, I go to prepare a place for you. And if I go and prepare a place for you, I will come again and receive you to Myself: that where I am, there you may be also" (John 14:2, 3).

Only by knowing and loving God can you have the hope of seeing your child again. God loved your child. He loves you. He loves all His children. He doesn't turn away from us. We turn away from Him. Even when we stray, He is constantly wooing us back to Him. Do you ever feel in your spirit that the direction you are taking is not the right one and change your mind? The still small voice of the Holy Spirit is gently calling you back to Him. I encourage you to yield to His voice and let Him minister to you. Don't forget, He gave His son for your life. If you have lost a child, you have a keener understanding of what that cost Him than someone who has never lost a child.

***

"For God so loved the world that He gave His only begotten Son, that whoever believes in Him should not perish but have everlasting life" (John 3:16).

***

"But God commendeth His love toward us, in that, while we were yet sinners, Christ died for us" (Romans 5:8).

***

Being angry with God won't remove the pain and suffering from your broken heart. Anger toward God will only prolong your pain. He is the only one that can heal your pain and give you hope.

Speaking to Martha, Lazarus's sister, Jesus said to her, "I am the resurrection and the life, He who believes in Me, though he may die, he shall live. And whoever lives and believes in Me shall never die. Do you believe this?" (John 11:25-26).

***

"For God so loved the world that He gave His only begotten Son, that whoever believes in Him should not perish but have everlasting life" (John 3:16).

***

God will never force Himself on you. You can look for comfort in other ways. Every other way will only be a temporary fix. There will always be a void in your heart that only God can fill with His saving grace, love, and hope.

I have watched the faces of those who chose to stay angry with God. They were sad faces, almost lifeless. Long term anger can also lead to health problems, insomnia, and depression.

When we lose someone we love we often begin looking for someone to blame. We almost always blame the wrong person, ourselves, others, or God.

Remember when Adam ate from the forbidden tree? Immediately he blamed Eve. It wasn't Eve's fault or God's. Adam gave into temptation. That temptation came from the devil. Yes, I said devil. Throughout the scriptures God speaks to us about the devil who thought he was equal with God or could be greater. God cast him out of heaven and he took a third of the angels with him. They have a limited time on earth and they only want to rob, steal, and destroy.

You can say I don't believe in the devil or demons, but if you do, you will also have to say that you do not believe in the Bible. The Bible is full of scriptures mentioning the devil. It is not a fairytale. If you study the Old Testament you will find many prophecies that were fulfilled that prove the Bible is the inspired Word of God. People are so fast to believe everything written in history books, but argue against believing the Bible whose prophecies have come to pass. If our forefathers had studied the Bible they wouldn't have needed to learn the earth was round from Magellan. God told us that in Isaiah 40:22.

***

"It is He who sits above the circle of the earth, and its inhabitants are like grasshoppers, Who stretches out the heavens like a curtain, And spreads them out like a tent to dwell in" (Isaiah 40:22).

***

God often gets blamed for what the devil is doing. We live in a fallen world, a world that is not perfect. In this world there will be trials, tribulations, sickness, disease, and death; but death has been conquered. When Jesus was crucified and rose again on the third day, He conquered death. Now death is a new beginning. When our physical body dies, our spiritual body goes to be with the Lord in heaven. It helps to remember where are loved one is going and that we will see them again. This is a time when you need to lean into God, not away from God. He is the One who heals the brokenhearted.

***

"He heals the brokenhearted and binds up their wounds, He counts the number of the stars; He calls them all by name" (Psalms 147:3).

***

How great is our God! He is the One who comforts those who mourn.

***

"Blessed are those who mourn, for they shall be comforted" (Mathew 5:4).

***

To those the devil is tormenting with guilt in their loved ones death, you need to know that God decides our times. Their days were not numbered according to what you would do or not do, or if you did this or said that. When we are at the judgment seat in court, does the judge ask you, "what did your parents do to get you here?" Does he judge you on your actions or theirs? What other people do can only affect us as much as we let them. We don't have that much power. We are not the ones in control. We can only do what we know to do. Stop asking yourself the 'what if questions'.

***

I would like to help you experience God's intimacy by leading you in a prayer to invite Jesus to become Lord and Savior of your life. A simple child like prayer said from your heart is all you need to do to invite God's Holy Spirit to come into your life and you will experience His love and guidance in a new and real way. Say these words if you can make them your own.

"Heavenly Father I believe that you love me so much that you sent your only begotten Son, Jesus, to come to this earth to pay my sin debt in full, once and for all. I accept your free gift of Christ's sacrifice of His life for mine. I want Jesus to come into my heart by way of His Holy Spirit and I choose to make Him Lord of my life. Holy Spirit please guide me in all that I do going forward. Help me to live regret free. Help me to desire to know you more. Please comfort me in this time of grieving. I need you. Thank you for loving me enough to suffer and die in my place. Amen."

If you said that prayer, I encourage you to write today's date here.

***

You will want to remember this day.

Your decision to ask Jesus to live in your heart will be the best decision you ever made. The angels are celebrating you in heaven.

Made in the USA
Columbia, SC
12 March 2024

32601010R00035